THOMAS ALVA
EDISON

GREAT AMERICAN INVENTOR

SPECIAL LIVES IN HISTORY THAT BECOME

Signature LIVES

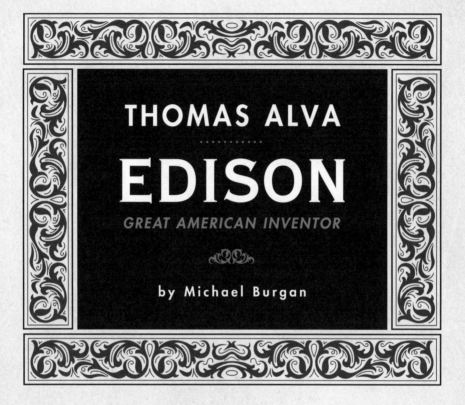

THOMAS ALVA

EDISON

GREAT AMERICAN INVENTOR

by Michael Burgan

Content Adviser: Louis Carlat, Ph.D.,
Thomas A. Edison Papers,
Rutgers, The State University of New Jersey

Reading Adviser: Rosemary G. Palmer, Ph.D.,
Department of Literacy, College of Education,
Boise State University

COMPASS POINT BOOKS ✦ MINNEAPOLIS, MINNESOTA

Compass Point Books
3109 West 50th Street, #115
Minneapolis, MN 55410

Visit Compass Point Books on the Internet at *www.compasspointbooks.com*
or e-mail your request to *custserv@compasspointbooks.com*

Editor: Sue Vander Hook
Page Production: Noumenon Creative
Photo Researchers: Marcie C. Spence and Svetlana Zhurkin
Cartographer: XNR Productions, Inc.
Library Consultant: Kathleen Baxter

Art Director: Jaime Martens
Creative Director: Keith Griffin
Editorial Director: Carol Jones
Managing Editor: Catherine Neitge

Library of Congress Cataloging-in-Publication Data
Burgan, Michael
  Thomas Alva Edison: Great American Inventor / by Michael Burgan.
    p. cm.—(Signature lives)
  Includes bibliographical references and index.
  ISBN-13: 978-0-7565-1884-4 (hardcover)
  ISBN-10: 0-7565-1884-9 (hardcover)
  ISBN-13: 978-0-7565-2099-1 (paperback)
  ISBN-10: 0-7565-2099-1 (paperback)
  1. Edison, Thomas A. (Alva), 1847–1931—Juvenile literature. 2. Electric
Engineers—United States—Biography—Juvenile literature. 3. Inventors—
United States—Biography—Juvenile literature. I. Title. II. Series.
  TK140.E3B875 2006
  621.3092—dc22   2006003000

Signature Lives

MODERN AMERICA

Starting in the late 19th century, advancements in all areas of human activity transformed an old world into a new and modern place. Inventions prompted rapid shifts in lifestyle, and scientific discoveries began to alter the way humanity viewed itself. Beginning with World War I, warfare took place on a global scale, and ideas such as nationalism and communism showed that countries were taking a larger view of their place in the world. The combination of all these changes continues to produce what we know as the modern world.

Table of Contents

THE WIZARD OF MENLO PARK 9

SCIENTIST AND ENTREPRENEUR 15

ON THE MOVE 25

THE BUSINESS OF INVENTING 35

THE INVENTION FACTORY 43

A BETTER LIGHTBULB 55

LIGHTING UP THE WORLD 63

CAPTURING MOVEMENT 71

CREATIVE BUSINESSMAN 81

AMERICAN HERO 89

LIFE AND TIMES 96

LIFE AT A GLANCE 102

ADDITIONAL RESOURCES 103

GLOSSARY 105

SOURCE NOTES 106

SELECT BIBLIOGRAPHY 108

INDEX 109

IMAGE CREDITS 112

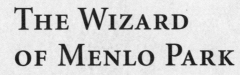

1 THE WIZARD OF MENLO PARK

❧❦❧

Under his arm, Thomas Alva Edison carried an invention unlike anything else in the world. He was on his way to visit the New York City office of *Scientific American,* a leading magazine on science and technology. Edison strolled into the office and placed the small device on a table. At least a dozen people gathered round. He turned a crank on one end of the apparatus. Suddenly, sound poured out of a cylinder that stuck out of the middle. The workers were amazed to hear Edison's voice come out of the contraption. One reporter wrote:

> *The machine inquired as to our health, asked how we liked the phonograph, informed us that it was very well, and bid us a cordial good night.*

Thomas Alva Edison (1847–1931) with his phonograph

The original phonograph was patented by Thomas Alva Edison in 1878.

It was December 1877, and no one had ever heard a machine speak so clearly. Edison had recorded his own voice, and the device played it back. Thus, the phonograph was born. The first public display of Edison's new invention was over, but his work was just beginning.

The phonograph had many exciting possibilities. A friend of Edison's wrote:

> Some of the great singers will be induced to sing into the ear of the phonograph ... [and] nothing will be easier than to catch the sounds of the waves on the beach ... the voices of animals ... or even the tumult of battle.

Edison wanted many people to buy his invention. But he also imagined many practical uses for his phonograph. He hoped it would provide a way for blind people to listen to recorded books. Children could listen to the alphabet and get an early start on reading. Toys would talk and sing. Family members could record their family history for future generations, and a dying person might preserve some last words or wishes. "In fact," Edison wrote, "its utility [uses] will be endless."

His discoveries didn't stop at this recording device. Driven by his curiosity to understand the world, Edison was constantly thinking and juggling several new inventions at a time. He filled numerous notebooks with ideas and sketches. With a desire to make life easier for everyone, he searched for ways to improve what he and others had already created. Those efforts would lead to 1,093 U.S. patents being granted to him for his ideas and inventions.

Throughout 1878, Edison showed his phonograph to news-

A patent is an exclusive right granted by a government. It protects a person's idea or invention so no one else can use it, make it, or sell it. Once Edison held a patent on something, businesses had to pay him to use it. Sometimes, Edison had to go to court to stop companies that were selling items that used his ideas without his permission. Edison's 1,093 patents are the most that any one person has ever held. Not all of his patents, however, led to inventions that were actually produced. Some were merely ideas or improvements of existing devices.

paper reporters and businessmen. Magazines and newspapers published articles and printed pictures of him and his amazing invention. News of Edison and his phonograph spread throughout New York City and then across the country.

Arc lights were used to light large outdoor spaces, like New York's Madison Square, in the early 1880s. Edison improved the lightbulb so it could be used indoors and last for hours.

Edison became well-known. He would one day become a popular hero for developing many other inventions, including an improved telegraph, an electric pen, an electronic vote recorder, a stock ticker, and a lightbulb that lasted hundreds of hours. His research lab in Menlo Park, New Jersey, would employ a crew of brilliant scientists, inventors, and mechanics. It would be remembered as one of the greatest research labs in the world.

Fascinated with capturing motion on film, Edison would also build a film studio in West Orange, New Jersey, where some of the world's first motion pictures would be recorded.

One newspaper article gave Edison a fitting nickname—the Wizard of Menlo Park. The name would stick with this great American inventor for the rest of his life. ℘

2 SCIENTIST AND ENTREPRENEUR

Chapter

❧❧❧

In the 1840s, when Thomas Alva Edison was born, life was not easy for many Americans. Farmers and factory workers put in long hours. On cold nights, families gathered around fireplaces for warmth. Candles and lanterns provided the only light. Still, the country was growing, and people who worked hard usually provided decent incomes for their families.

Samuel and Nancy Edison and their seven children lived in Milan, Ohio. Their youngest child, Thomas Alva Edison, was born on February 11, 1847. They called him Al. At the time of Al's birth, the town of Milan was experiencing a boom as a popular port for shipping grain to distant markets. A man-made canal connected the town to a nearby river and Lake Erie.

Young Edison in his railway uniform

Samuel Edison
(1804–1896)

Nancy Edison
(1810–1871)

By the early 1850s, however, Milan's economy was declining. Railroads were replacing ships and transporting more and more goods and crops. In 1854, Samuel Edison moved his family to Port Huron, Michigan. The town hummed with sawmills that turned trees into building materials. There Samuel joined many others who worked in the lumber industry.

The Edisons lived in a large two-story house. The family wasn't poor, but Samuel's income was often unsteady. At times, the family rented out rooms in their home to make extra income. Samuel found another creative way to earn money. He built a tower on his property that provided a good view of the countryside and Lake Huron. He charged people to climb the tower and look at the scenery. The Edisons also raised crops and sold vegetables in town. Young

Al often helped with farming tasks.

For a while, Al attended private school, but his father couldn't always pay the fee. Even public schools cost money, so Al didn't attend until he was about 12 or 13 years old. In the meantime, his mother educated him at home. "My mother was the making of me," he later remembered. "My mother taught me how to read good books quickly and correctly."

Al was an enthusiastic reader. He enjoyed books about history, science, physics, literature, and philosophy. Because he was such a curious child, he often performed chemical and electrical experiments at home. Once he strung a telegraph wire between his house and a friend's. The boys communicated with each other by using Morse code, a series of short and long electrical pulses that represent letters and numbers.

When Al wasn't studying, he swam and sailed small boats in the summer. In the winter, he skated and sledded. In the 1850s, children often took jobs to help their families earn money. In 1859, Al

Morse code was originally sent as electrical pulses along a telegraph wire. A short pulse, called a dot or a dit, was written on paper like this: •. A long pulse, called a dash or a dah, looked like this: ▬. There was a gap, or silence, between letters, words, and sentences when no pulse was sent. The word hello looks like this in Morse code:

•••• • •▬•• •▬•• ▬ ▬ ▬

h   e   l   l   o

The original code became known as Railroad or American Morse code, which is rarely used today.

convinced his mother to let him work for the Grand Trunk Railway, which ran through Port Huron. He became a newsboy who sold newspapers, candy, and other items to passengers on the train.

Edison was a newsboy and a candy butcher, a common term for boys who sold candy and other items to railroad passengers.

Al was interested in many things and took opportunities to learn and explore. Sometimes he watched the engineers drive the locomotive, and once, an engineer let him take over the controls. He

also read books whenever he had time. In Detroit, the train's last stop, he discovered a library. He spent hours reading books there while he waited for the return train.

In addition to his job with the railroad, Al had his own business in Port Huron. Before he took his newsboy job, he had set up two small stands in town, where he sold fruits, vegetables, and magazines. When he went to work for the railroad, he hired two boys to run the stands for him.

In April 1861, when Al was 14, the Civil War broke out. Major battles were being fought in the South, and residents of Michigan were eager for news. Al found a way to help these curious people and also make a lot of money. In 1862, after the Battle of Shiloh, Al doubled the price of a newspaper from a nickel to a dime, and no one complained. At each train stop, he raised the price. By the time he returned to Port Huron that day, the newspaper cost 25 cents, and everybody bought one.

After that success, Al decided to print his own newspaper. With the help of a train conductor, he set up a printer in a baggage car. The *Weekly Herald*, as it was called, published news about the railroad and towns along the route. He sold several hundred copies a week. In addition to his newspaper business, Al also used an empty train car to conduct his chemistry experiments. However, that hobby ended quickly in the summer of 1862 when a chemical spilled and started a fire. A conductor burned his leg putting out the blaze and then angrily smacked Al on the ears.

About this time, Al began losing his hearing. Some thought the conductor's blow to his ear damaged his hearing, but no one ever knew for sure. His hearing got continually worse, but later he considered his deafness a positive thing. "Deafness probably drove me to reading," he wrote, and "freedom from such [small] talk gave me an opportunity to think out my problems."

Thomas Alva Edison as a young boy

The train conductor who put out the chemical fire forced Al to shut down the *Weekly Herald*. But soon Al started another paper, the *Paul Pry*. According to Al's partner in this venture, the paper was filled with hot stuff that offended some readers. One time, an angry reader punched Al. Someone else pushed the young publisher into a river. After this, Al lost interest in publishing. But he found another passion to fill his time—telegraphy. He was fascinated with sending and receiving messages through a telegraph line.

He already knew the basics, thanks to his homemade telegraph wire and what he had learned from the railroad operators. In the fall of 1862, Al trained with James MacKenzie, a professional telegraph operator. MacKenzie wanted to do something special for Al, who once ran onto the tracks

Edison once rescued MacKenzie's child.

During the Civil War, Union telegraph operators used crude shelters to house their equipment.

and rescued MacKenzie's son from a runaway freight car. Al received telegraphy lessons as a reward for saving the boy's life.

Within several months, Al knew enough to become

a telegraph operator for Western Union. He set up his telegraph in a jewelry store in Port Huron. Sending and receiving telegrams didn't always fill his time, however. So he read books and studied the tools the jeweler used to repair clocks and watches.

The jeweler later recalled:

[Al] had plenty of time to experiment and tinker. And in doing so, was a great annoyance to my workmen.

The teenager was learning skills that would later help him as an inventor. ✍

The telegraph and railroad industries developed at the same time in the United States. Telegraph companies strung their lines along railways, and railroad companies used the telegraph to keep track of their trains. When Edison took his first job in telegraphy, Western Union was one of the major U.S. telegraph companies. By 1870, it dominated the industry.

3 ON THE MOVE

‮৲‮

At the age of 16, Thomas Alva Edison joined thousands of other young Americans, mostly single men, who went from city to city as telegraph operators. His first assignment was working for the Grand Trunk Railway in Stratford Junction, a small town in Ontario, Canada. Edison constantly tried to improve his skills at sending and receiving telegraph messages by Morse code.

Edison worked the night shift, and during the day he read books and performed experiments. Since he was so interested in learning and experimenting, he didn't sleep very much. Sometimes he took catnaps at work.

Edison wasn't in Stratford Junction very long. One night he failed to tell a conductor that his train

Samuel Morse (1791–1872) invented the Morse code system used to send messages by telegraph.

should not leave the railroad station. The engineer drove his train out of the station and ended up on the same track as a train going in the opposite direction. Although the trains didn't collide, Edison's bosses were angry. Edison slipped out of Stratford and hurried home to Port Huron before they could fire him.

His next jobs took him to Adrian, Michigan, and Fort Wayne, Indiana, where he worked for a short time as a telegraph operator for railroad companies. In 1864, he was again working for Western Union in a bustling telegraph office in Indianapolis, Indiana. He hoped to be promoted to press-wire operator, someone who received incoming news reports for local newspapers. These operators were the fastest in the business, and they were paid well.

In his spare time, Edison worked on his first invention—a device that printed the electrical impulses of Morse code as dots and dashes on a strip of paper. No longer would a telegraph operator have to write the message by hand. The device worked well, but it didn't impress the other operators. One of them later remembered how the workers made fun of his attempts to be something better than an operator. But that didn't stop Edison from searching for new and better ways to do his job.

A little luck and his own determination helped him get the promotion he desired. One night, most of the other operators got drunk, and the usual press-wire operator didn't show up for work. Edison decided to fill in for him. Edison did such a good job that his manager promoted him to press-wire operator.

By spring 1866, Edison was on his way to Western Union's office in Cincinnati, Ohio, where he received another promotion. Throughout that year, he also worked in Memphis, Tennessee, and Louisville, Kentucky. As always, he tried to improve his telegraph skills and still find time for experimenting.

The Morse telegraph key was connected by a wire to the battery-operated telegraph apparatus.

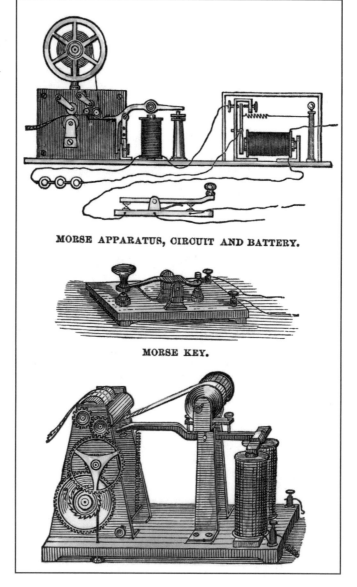

MORSE APPARATUS, CIRCUIT AND BATTERY.

MORSE KEY.

But in 1867, an experiment with a battery cost Edison his job in Louisville. Acid from the battery leaked and ate a hole in the floor, which angered his boss.

Edison returned to the telegraph office in Cincinnati and continued to work on devices that would improve the telegraph. He experimented with relays, repeaters, and duplexes. Relays used electromagnets to send electrical signals through a wire. Repeaters relied on batteries to boost the strength of the electrical signal as it traveled through the telegraph wire. A duplex allowed two messages to go in opposite directions on one telegraph wire at the same time. Edison drew sketches of his ideas in a notebook and built a small workshop, where he made the parts he needed for his invention.

> *The introduction of the telegraph changed the world of journalism. Before the telegraph, news might take weeks to reach a small-town paper. News could travel only as fast as people or animals could deliver it. The telegraph let people share information almost immediately. Companies called wire services provided stories for local newspapers by sending telegraphs with the latest news. A wire service called the Associated Press, founded in 1848, still exists today. It employs thousands of people in hundreds of locations around the world. News stories are now transmitted digitally by computers.*

Life was not all work for Edison, however. He also had a mischievous side. In the bathroom at the Cincinnati Western Union office, he rigged some wires and a battery. When workers washed their hands, they received a jolt of electricity—not enough to hurt, but plenty to make them jump a bit. Edison hid above the ceiling and watched what was going on through a small hole he had made. There he laughed and enjoyed his practical joke. Throughout his life, Edison always enjoyed making others laugh at his pranks and clever stories.

At the end of 1867, Edison returned to his hometown of Port Huron, Michigan. At the age of 20, he was now a highly skilled telegraph operator and a successful inventor. Few people knew about his skills. That changed, however, when Edison published his first technical article in the April 1868 *Telegrapher*, a magazine for telegraph operators. His article explained the duplex, which he called a double transmitter. The editors of the magazine called his design "interesting ... and ingenious [creative]."

By the time the article was published, Edison had moved to Boston, Massachusetts, to work for Western Union as a press-wire operator. He traveled by train for four days to get there and hadn't slept much when he arrived. He later wrote, "I ... did not present a very fresh or stylish appearance." Edison never cared much about how he looked, and he often greeted visitors in rumpled, dirty clothes. But his skills more than made up for his appearance.

Boston provided a good climate for inventing. Many businesses relied on telegraphy to send mes-

Tremont Street in Boston, Massachusetts, in the 1860s

sages quickly to other businesses. They often sought ways to send messages faster and more cheaply. There were also many investors in Boston who hoped to make money on promising new inventions.

In his spare time, Edison continued to work on ways to improve telegraphy, and he applied for patents. He knew how important it was to get patents to guarantee that no one else could use his ideas or inventions. With a patent, Edison would be the only one who could make money from his creations.

In June 1869, Edison received his first U.S. patent for an electrical device that would record votes for members of Congress. Lawmakers, however, preferred the slower way of recording votes by hand so they had time to persuade others to vote their way. Edison never made any of the vote recorders.

Edison's improved stock ticker

Now Edison turned his attention to improving a machine called a ticker. Another inventor had made

this printing telegraph that recorded stock prices on a strip of paper. It was called a ticker for the tick-tick sound it made when it was printing. Bankers and investors who bought and sold stocks relied on tickers to receive news about the price of stocks. Edison's improvements made it faster and more efficient.

Although Edison was serious about his work, he still brought humor to the places he worked. At the Boston telegraph office, he entertained co-workers with a bug zapper. When a cockroach stepped on a strip of foil connected to a battery, the insect died in a puff of smoke. But when a client became annoyed with his fun-loving ways, Edison was given a less-important job.

Edison decided to resign from his Western Union job to devote himself to inventing. A short note appeared in the *Telegrapher*: "T.A. Edison has resigned his situation [position] in the Western Union office, Boston, Mass., and will devote his time to bringing out his inventions." Inventing was no longer just a hobby—it was now his career. 🖎

Prior to the invention of the stock ticker, stock prices were hand-written and hand-delivered. Edison's machine received stock prices by telegraph and printed them on a thin strip of paper called ticker tape. It was readable text, not in the dots and dashes of Morse code, and included the company's name and the current price of the company's stock. The machine printed one character per second. Often, used ticker tape was thrown from windows above parades to celebrate a significant event such as the end of a war. These became known as ticker-tape parades.

4 THE BUSINESS OF INVENTING

During the first part of 1869, Edison convinced a large Boston bank to use his improved stock ticker. It wasn't long before other customers were asking him to install them at their offices so they could stay up-to-date on current stock prices. Edison also sold some of his customers the magnetograph, a telegraph that didn't need a battery. Some customers disliked batteries since they could leak dangerous chemicals, as Edison had already discovered.

Edison also continued to work on his duplex telegraph and hoped to sell it to large telegraph companies. One New York company asked him to set up a 400-mile (640-kilometer) connection between New York City and Rochester, New York. Even though his attempts to send two messages at the same time

In the 1870s, telegraph wires were connected to buildings like the New York City Post Office.

on one wire failed, Edison learned some things about New York. The city had many potential customers and investors who were willing to spend money on new inventions.

By spring 1869, Edison was living in New York City. He met another telegraph operator and inventor named Franklin Pope who worked for the Gold and Stock Reporting Telegraph Company. It wasn't long before the two men became business partners and formed their own company. They named it Pope, Edison & Company.

In February 1870, another company offered Edison money to develop his inventions. He would receive $10,000 plus enough to set up his own shop where he could experiment and make things. Edison agreed and established the Newark Telegraph Works in Newark, New Jersey, located across the Hudson River from New York City. Later that year, Pope, Edison & Co. went out of business.

Marshall Lefferts, president of Gold and Stock, also wanted Edison to work on a new invention. It was called automatic telegraphy. With this system, a telegraph operator punched the dots and dashes of Morse code onto a strip of paper. The operator then fed the strip into something called a transmitter, which turned on an electrical current whenever it detected a hole in the paper. This system of sending a telegraph message was much faster than when an operator tapped out the dots and dashes by hand with a telegraph key.

Lefferts became Edison's good friend and helped him learn better ways to file and receive patents for his ideas and inventions. He described the inventor as "a genius and a very fiend for work." Edison hired brilliant scientists and mechanics to help him. Several new investors joined him as partners, and business was good.

In a letter home to his parents in October 1870, Edison wrote that he could afford to send them money if they needed it. Although some say he was bragging, Edison wrote that he had "a Large amount of business to attend to. I have one shop which Employs 18 men and am Fitting up another which will Employ over 150 men."

Mary Stilwell
(1855–1884)

For the next several years, Edison focused on automatic telegraphy and a device that would print a telegraph message on paper. But he also found time for 16-year-old Mary Stilwell, who worked for his company. Although 24-year-old Edison hadn't known Mary very long, he asked her to marry him. Mary's mother agreed, and they were married on Christmas Day, 1871.

Edison was disappointed to learn that Mary didn't share his interest in inventing. But Mary respected Edison and "thought him almost a god." On February 18, 1873, their first child—a girl named Marion Estelle—was born. Edison spent most of his time in his shop, often missing dinner and other family events. Later, Marion said that her "father's work always came first." Still, Edison spent a great deal of time with his daughter. He nicknamed her Dot for one of the Morse code symbols used to send telegraph messages.

Edison's daughter, Marion Estelle (1872–1965), at the age of 8

Edison constantly needed money to continue his work. Investors were harder to find when the U.S. economy declined sharply after 1873. But Edison was lucky enough to get acquainted with one of the country's richest investors, Jay Gould. He owned many railroad lines and Gould's Atlantic and Pacific Telegraph Company, which competed with Western Union.

Gould wanted Edison's new invention, the

quadruplex, for his telegraph company. He paid Edison $30,000 for the right to use it. The device could send four telegraph messages at a time, two in each direction, on a single wire. Gould also received the rights to Edison's automatic telegraph. In 1875, Edison briefly worked for Gould's company, but he preferred working for himself in his own shop. Any money he made went right back into more research and inventions.

Edison spent many hours each day in his shop.

Edison sketched his quadruplex and made notes about his new invention that could send four messages simultaneously on one telegraph wire.

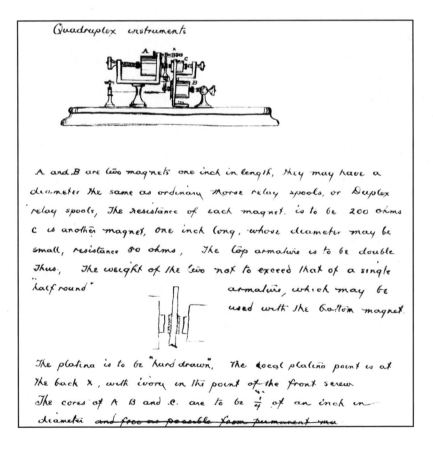

Quadruplex instruments

A and B are two magnets one inch in length, they may have a diameter the same as ordinary Morse relay spools, or Duplex relay spools, The resistance of each magnet is to be 200 ohms C is another magnet, one inch long, whose diameter may be small, resistance 80 ohms, The top armature is to be double Thus, The weight of the two not to exceed that of a single half round · armature, which may be used with the bottom magnet.

The platina is to be "hard drawn", The local platina point is at the back x, with ivory in the point of the front screw The cores of A B and C are to be $\frac{1}{4}$ of an inch in diameter and free as possible from permanent ma

Edison spent countless hours throughout his life experimenting in his laboratories.

He enjoyed the excitement of discovering new things. During one experiment, he saw unusual sparks coming from a magnet. How could there be sparks when it wasn't attached to a source of electricity? He believed that this source of energy, which he called the etheric force, could be used to send telegraph messages without wires.

His discovery would one day be the foundation for radio communication. Fourteen years later, in 1889, a man by the name of Heinrich Hertz would prove the existence of these radio waves.

Edison's experiments also included work on acoustic tele-graphy, a new device that used sound to send a telegraph mes-sage. He made good progress, but his greatest accomplishments were yet to come. ℘

Radio waves, like light waves, are a form of energy and constantly surround Earth. In the 1890s, Italian inventor Guglielmo Marconi experimented with radio waves and learned they could be sent over long distances. As Edison had suspected, Morse code could be sent through the air without wires. Marconi invented wireless tele-graph, which was the basis for the radio.

5 THE INVENTION FACTORY

෴

In March 1876, Edison and his family moved to Menlo Park, New Jersey. Edison liked the spot because it was in the country but still close to businesses and investors in New York City. With the help of his 72-year-old father, Edison built what he called an invention factory. The world had never seen anything like it before. The two-story wood building resembled a barn, but it was a well-equipped laboratory that would produce world-changing inventions.

On one floor, Edison and about 25 assistants researched, mixed chemicals, and tinkered with electrical devices. On the other floor was a machine shop, where mechanics developed the inventions that Edison and his team designed. Edison hired many employees to work at the lab, and he organized them to

Edison used profits from the sale of his inventions to build and improve his laboratories.

work as an efficient team. Chemists, mathematicians, engineers, and machinists all worked on different parts of the same invention.

Edison's top assistant was Charles Batchelor. James Adams was a lab assistant, and John Kruesi was the main mechanic. They helped Edison perfect some of his most famous inventions. His strong research and development team became a model that businesses follow even today. Edison said he hoped to produce a "minor invention every ten days and a big thing every six months or so." He wasn't boasting—he always believed hard work would lead to success.

Two months before the Edisons moved to Menlo Park, the couple had a son, Thomas Alva Edison Jr., born on January 10, 1876. Edison called him Dash, a nickname that reminded him of the Morse code symbol. Now his children were Dot and Dash. Another son, William Leslie, would be born in 1878.

Mary and the children rarely saw Edison, who spent most of his waking hours in his shop or vast

Charles Batchelor (1845–1910) came to the United States from England in 1870 to work for a textile manufacturer. He met Edison and became his top laboratory assistant and business partner for more than 30 years. Edison called him Batch and gave him the title chief experimental assistant. A talented experimenter, Batchelor tested and improved many of Edison's most important inventions.

library. Although he only slept four or five hours a night, he sometimes took catnaps during the day on a cot in his lab. "Sleep is like a drug," he said. "Take too much at a time and it makes you dopey. You lose time and opportunities."

At Edison's nearby factory, his employees were busy making another invention—the electric pen. With this device, powered by a small motor, a writer could cut words onto a piece of paper.

Thomas Alva Edison Jr. (1876–1935)

The paper then served as a stencil for making copies. The stencil was placed over a blank sheet of paper. Using a hand roller covered with ink, a person could make a printed copy of the document. One employee later wrote that the pen "could be found in the government offices in Washington D.C., in every city and state offices, and in such far-away lands as Australia, New Zealand, China ... and elsewhere."

William Leslie Edison (1878–1937)

The electric pen had a motor that pressed the tip down 133 times per second, making a stencil from which hundreds of copies could be made.

The electric pen was a success. But Edison was interested more in acoustic telegraphy. Another inventor—Alexander Graham Bell—would be the first to send sound through a wire, however. In the summer of 1876, Bell spoke into a device, and sound traveled through a wire. At the other end, his assistant heard his words.

Bell received the first patent for this invention— the telephone. But Edison quickly joined the race with many other scientists to improve it. Bell's phone used the same device to transmit and receive sound. The signal was weak, making it hard to hear the message on the other end. Edison and his assistants designed a transmitter to work with Bell's receiver. It had a much stronger electrical current, which made spoken words louder and clearer.

Edison's transmitter used a substance called carbon. Once Edison discovered that carbon was the key, he gave Batchelor the job of finding out what kind of carbon worked best. Batchelor experimented and found the answer inside a lamp. At that time, kerosene was often used as lamp fuel. When kerosene burned, it left a film of black carbon inside the lamp's glass chimney.

In order to test the carbon, Edison built a small building and filled it with dozens of burning kerosene lamps. Workers scraped the carbon, called lampblack, off the glass and formed it into small buttonlike objects. These carbon buttons were then tested inside Edison's transmitters.

Alexander Graham Bell (1847–1922) was raised in Scotland. As a teenager, he experimented with sounds made by human speech. At the age of 21, he began teaching hearing-impaired children how to speak at Susannah Hull's school for deaf children in London. Two years later, his family emigrated to Ontario, Canada, and then to Boston, Massachusetts, where Bell taught at two schools for deaf children. While experimenting with a telegraph in 1876, he developed a device that transmitted someone's voice. The first complete sentence he spoke through his apparatus was "Mr. Watson, come here; I want to see you." This led to the creation of the first working telephone. Edison's work helped to improve the telephone and make it a commercial success.

The experiments with the transmitter didn't always go well. In 1877, Edison wrote to his father in Port Huron, "I am having pretty hard luck with my speaking telegraph [telephone], but I think it is O.K. now." He also noted that he was "very hard up for cash." But he finally perfected and marketed his transmitter, and his personal finances improved. That year, Western Union went into the telephone business. Edison sold his patent rights for his telephone transmitter to Western Union for $100,000—equivalent to about $1.8 million today.

While Edison was working on the telephone transmitter, he was also experimenting with a separate device that would record sound. He called it a phonograph, which comes from two Greek words that mean "writing" and "sound." Although Edison's hearing had worsened with age, he remained fascinated by sound.

The stylus, or needle, was at the heart of Edison's new recording device. Sound vibrations caused the stylus to move and cut grooves into wax-covered paper. To play back the sound, a second stylus moved over the grooves in the paper and caused a thin piece of material called a diaphragm to vibrate. These vibrations created the same sound originally recorded on the paper.

Edison discovered that the waxy paper wasn't working very well. He switched to tin foil wrapped around a small cylinder. When he turned a crank to make the cylinder rotate, the stylus moved along it. He later noted that the foil "easily received and recorded the movements of the diaphragm."

In November 1877, Edison gave a drawing of his new machine to Kruesi, his main mechanic. About a week later, Kruesi presented Edison with the finished product. Edison spoke into a cylinder attached to the device—"Mary had a little lamb, its fleece was

Edison recorded his own voice on his phonograph.

white as snow, and everywhere that Mary went, the lamb was sure to go." With a turn of the crank, the phonograph played back his exact words. The men in the shop were amazed. Edison's invention worked on the first try.

The first phonograph was far from perfect or easy to use. Wrapping the foil around the cylinder could take several minutes. Turning the crank at the right speed took practice. The foil cylinder could only record for about 10 seconds, and the recording could only be played back two or three times before the steel stylus tore through the foil.

Eventually, Edison's phonograph had a large megaphone to increase the sound.

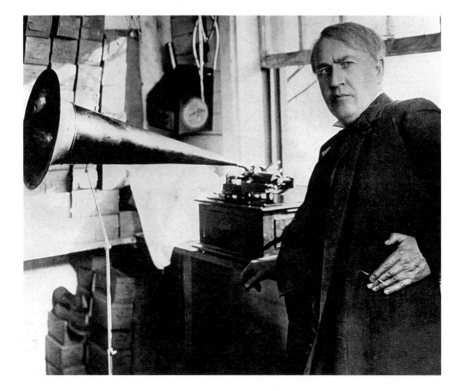

But Edison's machine could record and play back sound, and Edison was ready to show it to the world. He took the phonograph to the editors of *Scientific American*. After impressing them, he showed it to Western Union leaders and eagerly talked to reporters from all over the country. News about his invention spread quickly. Edison knew he had created something fantastic. He told one newspaper reporter:

This is my baby and I expect it to be a big feller and support me in my old age.

Some people purchased phonographs and traveled around the country demonstrating the device for a fee. People were fascinated with the contraption and willingly bought tickets to see and hear it at fairs and other public places. Edison received 20 percent of the profits.

Even though the public was excited about hearing a recorded voice, the phonograph still needed

In time, Edison became totally deaf in one ear and hard of hearing in the other. He considered his deafness a blessing. He didn't have to participate much in conversations, and he didn't hear the clacking sounds of co-workers' telegraphs. He believed his hearing impairment led to some of his greatest inventions. About the phonograph, he said, "Deafness, pure and simple, was responsible for the experimentation which perfected the machine." Later he admitted, "The telephone as we now know it might have been delayed if a deaf electrician had not undertaken the job of making it a practical thing."

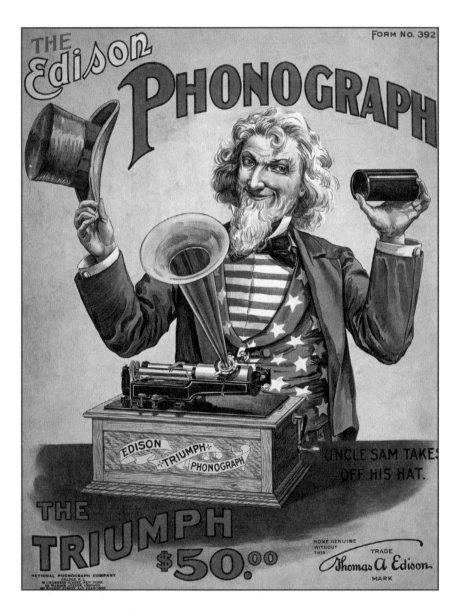

A poster advertisement featured Uncle Sam doffing his hat to Edison's fine invention.

improvement. It was expensive, hard to operate, and not widely available. After the wonder of hearing recorded sound wore off, few would pay again to see it. Edison had created something remarkable, but the world wasn't sure what to do with it.

Other inventors began making improvements to Edison's phonograph. They used wax instead of tin foil on the cylinder and a floating stylus instead of a rigid needle. When approached about working together with these inventors, Edison refused. He would later make many improvements of his own to the phonograph and establish the Edison Phonograph Company.

Newspapers and scientists praised Edison's work. One professor called him the greatest inventor of the age. Soon he was known as the Wizard of Menlo Park. Edison was not just an inventor. He was a hero and a celebrity. That fame would spread even further with his next great invention. ॐ

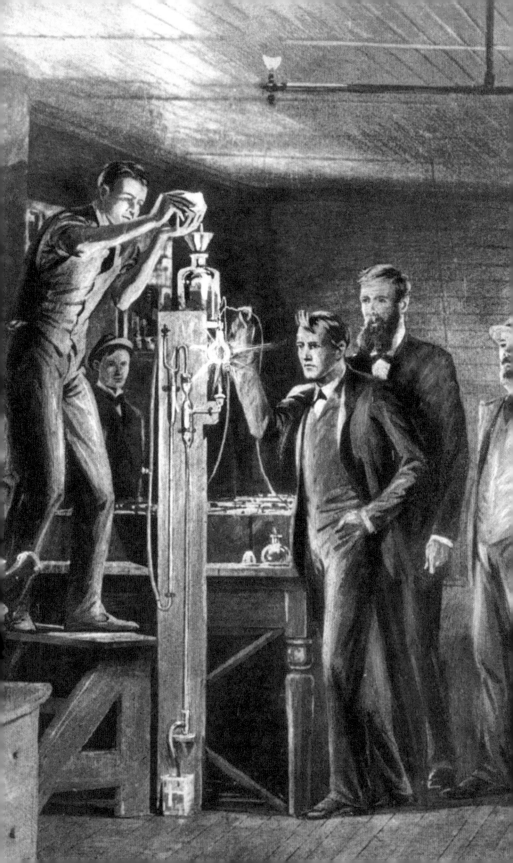

6

A BETTER LIGHTBULB

❧⌘❧

Edison loved to learn and experiment. An avid reader, he kept current with magazine articles about the latest technical and scientific advances around the world. He often talked with other inventors. In September 1878, he visited a Connecticut lab where work was being done on electric lighting. His visit encouraged him to talk to other scientists and read about lighting. Then Edison started a new project.

At that time, electric illumination was by arc lighting, which was used mostly outdoors. In this type of lighting system, two pieces of metal called electrodes were separated by a narrow gap. Electricity formed an arc across this gap, producing a bright spark of light. Because of the intense light, arc lamps were used mostly as streetlamps or in lighthouses.

Edison (center front) and others observed while Francis Jahl worked on a lightbulb in the Menlo Park lab.

Electric arc lighting was installed in Bridge Square in Minneapolis, Minnesota, and illuminated on February 28, 1883.

They were too bright for indoor use.

Inventors and scientists were experimenting with something called incandescent light. Inside an incandescent lightbulb, a thin wirelike material called a filament formed a curve with no gap. When electricity heated the filament, it glowed and created a soft light. The filament was suspended inside a glass bulb from which the air had been removed to form a partial vacuum. But the filament burned up quickly in incandescent bulbs. Edison created a lightbulb with a filament that didn't burn up as quickly. It also used less electricity to produce the same amount of light. One of the keys to his longer-lasting bulb was removing more air from the glass.

The source of electricity for these first lightbulbs was batteries. But soon, scientists and engineers were building dynamos, machines that would produce large amounts of electricity. In his visit to a Connecticut lab, Edison saw one of these huge dynamos at work. The invention excited him, and he wanted to produce a dynamo that was bigger and better than all the others. He envisioned electricity being sent over long distances and powering hundreds of lightbulbs at the same time.

Seeing the dynamo convinced Edison to devote his time to creating an electric source that would deliver electricity to homes and businesses everywhere. Always confident, Edison told one reporter he would create a bulb and a dynamo that would bring electricity to all of New York City in just a few weeks. People who wanted electric lights would pay to use the electricity. Someone told Edison he could make a fortune if his plan worked. "I don't care so much about making my fortune," Edison said, "as I do for getting ahead of the other fellows."

The Edison team began work on a dynamo that was more powerful than the one Edison had seen in Connecticut. Edison also erected a new building at Menlo Park, where his workers tested every aspect of electric lighting. They improved the vacuum inside the lightbulb and found the right material for a filament. Experiments with carbon helped them develop a better filament. Again, they conducted tests with carbon from the lampblack inside kerosene lamp chimneys. They rolled the carbon into thin threads to make a filament that would burn for hours.

By the end of 1879, Edison had strung up wires and lights throughout his shops and invited people to see his invention. One newspaper reported that hundreds of people traveled through stormy weather to marvel at Edison's latest creation. "Surging crowds filed into the laboratory, machine shop and private office of the scientist." Edison finally closed his shop to

Many people believe Edison invented the incandescent lightbulb. But the first one appeared around 1820 in France. Decades later, an English inventor named Joseph Swan also created a bulb. While Edison was perfecting the lightbulb, Swan and an American named William Sawyer were working on a similar one. When Edison filed for a patent, Sawyer filed a legal challenge. He claimed he already held a patent on a similar bulb. The U.S. Patent Office ruled in Sawyer's favor. But in 1889, a U.S. court overturned that decision and ruled that Edison's patent was valid.

Edison's incandescent electric light-bulb was invented in 1879.

the public, but he kept lights burning outside "so that those who come will not be disappointed."

Members of Edison's team continued to improve the filament until they created one that burned for hundreds of hours. Edison's next goal was to create a system that would light an entire city and carry electricity through wires over long distances. He hired new workers and looked for men educated in mathematics and chemistry.

It took Edison's team about two years to perfect the incandescent lightbulb. His workers also

In early 1880, Edison noticed layers of carbon building up inside the glass of his lightbulb. He couldn't explain how tiny bits of carbon were getting there. He finally realized that electrical current was carrying them from the filament to the inside surface. This meant that the current could travel through space without passing through a wire. This was later called the Edison Effect. Future scientists and inventors used their understanding of the Edison Effect to create radios and other electronic devices.

designed sockets, fuses, meters, and underground wires. All the pieces worked together to produce light. Edison then joined with his investors to form the Edison Electric Light Company.

Edison expected his employees to work hard, and he didn't pay well. He expected them to be like him—muckers, as he called them, who would get their hands dirty to achieve success. Many of the young men he hired only stayed with him a few years. But during that time, they learned from a master inventor. As one worker put it, "The privilege which I had being with this great man for six years was the greatest inspiration of my life."

By 1881, Edison and his family were again living in New York City, where Edison prepared to install his first public lighting system. Edison remembered the first time he had lived in New York:

> I had to walk the streets ... all night because I hadn't the price of a bed. And now think of it! I'm to occupy a whole house on Fifth Avenue!

The Edison home was in one of the best neighborhoods in the city. Edison soon set up lights in his grand home as an advertisement for the citywide electrical system he was planning. He wanted to sell people on his idea of electric lights in homes and offices. A *New York Herald* reporter once described Edison's vision: "We will make electric light so cheap that only the rich will be able to burn candles."

Investors continued to show interest in Edison's efforts. J. Pierpont Morgan, one of the most powerful bankers and businessmen in the United States, bought a small generator from Edison and had lights installed in his own home.

The banker said, "I think there is a good thing in this for parties [people] who ... introduce it properly into cities." Edison would do just that. Soon cities would be powered by dynamos and lit up with incandescent lights. ℘

American banker and financier J. Pierpont Morgan (1837–1913) supported Edison.

7 LIGHTING UP THE WORLD

Chapter

❦❧

Edison installed his first power station dynamo on Pearl Street near New York's financial district. On September 4, 1882, Edison and his investors gathered in Morgan's office to turn on a light that drew its power from the Pearl Street station. The lightbulb lit up; the system was working. A satisfied Edison told a reporter, "I have accomplished all I promised."

Edison was just beginning his mission to bring light to the world. Batchelor, his number-one assistant, was setting up electrical lighting in Paris, while another trusted assistant did the same in London. Edison's trained technicians were building power stations throughout Europe.

Factories worldwide bought power plants from Edison's company so they could have lights. In March

Edison's dynamo generated the first electrical lighting system in New York City.

> *Although Edison completed the first electric power system, he soon had a major competitor. In 1885, George Westinghouse (1846–1914) bought the patents for an electrical system that used alternating current (AC). This meant the electrical current changed direction rapidly as it flowed. AC generators produced electricity that could be sent efficiently over long distances. Edison's system used direct current (DC). The current only moved in one direction and could only travel short distances. Westinghouse's system became more popular, and Edison refused to switch to an AC system. He remained convinced that his system was the best way to power lights and other electrical devices. Today's electric power systems are AC.*

1883, Edison established a new company that focused on building power stations in towns all across the United States.

But in early 1884, Edison took time away from his work to travel with his family to Fort Myers, Florida. Mary enjoyed the vacation because she finally had her husband to herself. But she battled with physical problems, which seemed to affect her mental health.

After the family returned from their trip, Mary's health got worse. That August, she died unexpectedly. Edison was deeply saddened. Twelve-year-old Marion said her father was "shaking with grief, weeping and sobbing so he could hardly tell me that mother had died in the night." Edison now spent more time with Marion. She traveled with him on business trips and ran errands for him.

Edison also returned to inventing. But in 1885, he met 20-year-old Mina Miller. She was used to the world of inventing. Her father

Lewis Miller had made a million-dollar fortune designing farm equipment.

Thirty-eight-year-old Edison first saw Mina in New Orleans, Louisiana, and then began visiting her in Boston, where she attended school. Although she was much younger than Edison, she was well-educated and showed more interest in his work than Mary had.

Edison's second wife, Mina Miller Edison (1865–1947)

Edison taught Mina how to use Morse code so they could tap out secret messages to each other. One day, Edison tapped out a special message—he asked Mina to marry him. Mina used Morse code to reply with the word *yes*.

Mina Miller and Thomas Alva Edison were married on February 24, 1886. They spent their honeymoon in Fort Myers. They enjoyed observing and experimenting with sea life together. Edison told about "shock[ing] an oyster to see if it won't paralyze his shell muscle and make his shell fly open." The experiment failed. When they returned to New Jersey, Mina joined Edison in his lab to record the results of some of their experiments.

Glenmont, the home of Thomas and Mina Edison in West Orange, New Jersey

The Edison family then moved into a huge home in West Orange, New Jersey. The house and property were called Glenmont. Along with his lab, Edison had a large collection of books that was considered the most complete technical library in the United States in the 1890s. Mina quickly learned what Mary had known—work came first for Edison. He continued to work long hours in his lab and travel all over the country making business deals and speaking about scientific issues.

Edison's business empire was growing. His companies were making lightbulbs and dynamos and installing power systems. However, employees at one of his businesses, the Edison Machine Works, thought their wages were too low. For a time in 1886, several hundred of them went on strike, refusing to work. They demanded higher wages and the right to form a union, an organization that would help them receive fair wages and decent working conditions. Batchelor, who ran the company, agreed to raise their salaries but opposed the creation of a union. The workers accepted these terms. But soon Batchelor moved the company about 160 miles (256 km) away to a larger factory in Schenectady, New York, partly to get away from its dissatisfied workers in New York City.

In 1887, Edison began building a new laboratory in West Orange. He wanted "the best equipped & largest Laboratory extant [in existence]" where he could perfect "rapid & cheap development of an invention." The main building was three stories high and 250 feet (76 meters) long. Inside were two machine shops. Four other buildings were used for electrical and chemical experiments. At this new site, Edison said he could "build anything from a lady's watch to a Locomotive."

Edison now turned his attention to improving an old invention, the phonograph. He replaced the tin foil with a hollow wax tube that went over the metal

Edison's laboratory in West Orange, New Jersey

cylinder. After a recording was made, the top layer of the wax tube could be shaved off and used again. The new phonograph also had a better stylus and a motor to drive the cylinder. Now nearly deaf, Edison had a special way of "hearing" how his new phonograph sounded. Sometimes he bit down on the horn, which carried the sound from the diaphragm into the air. That way, he could feel the sound vibrations even if he couldn't hear them.

At the same time, Alexander Graham Bell's company was making improvements to Edison's design, calling it a graphophone. As Bell's company got ready to sell the graphophone to the public, Edison scrambled to beat Bell to the market and make a better phonograph. In June 1888, Edison ordered his men to work nonstop for three days to finish the improved phonograph. Finally, Edison was satisfied with the new device. He spent $250,000 of his own money to build a factory where the phonographs could be produced. By fall, his new phonographs were ready to sell.

Edison also revived another old idea: talking toys. In 1888, he asked Batchelor to design a doll with a small phonograph inside. Eventually, Edison's company made about 3,000 dolls that stood 22 inches (56 centimeters) tall. At the turn of a crank, the doll would speak.

Edison's $10 phonograph doll was called the greatest wonder of the age and described as a doll that could recite in a childish voice one of the well-known nursery rhymes. But customers weren't happy with the toy, and neither was Edison. Many of the dolls didn't work after a few days, and people returned them for refunds. Edison pulled them from the market and considered the talking doll a failure. But he was already thinking about his next great invention. 🐦

Edison's talking doll had an internal mechanism similar to the phonograph.

8 CAPTURING MOVEMENT

❧⟨∞⟩❧

Edison's fame as an inventor led many educated people to his West Orange lab. One visitor who arrived in 1888 was photographer Eadweard Muybridge. Recently, Muybridge had been experimenting with capturing motion with a series of cameras. He had set up a long row of cameras that photographed each stage of a horse in motion.

The cameras took pictures one after the other when the horse triggered a series of wires. When all the photographs were shown in rapid-fire succession, much like a flip book, it looked like the horse was running. His idea was the beginning of what became motion pictures, or movies.

In October 1888, Edison sketched out an idea for a machine that would record and show these moving

Edison recorded a sneeze as one of his first attempts to capture motion on film.

pictures. He called it a kinetoscope. The word came from two Greek words: *kineto*, meaning movement, and *scopos*, meaning to watch. He later wrote that he had "the hope of developing something that would do for the eye what the phonograph did for the ear." The kinetoscope looked a little like his first phonograph. In the center was a rotating cylinder. On film wrapped around the cylinder was a series of tiny pictures. As the cylinder turned, a person could watch the images "move" through a microscope placed close to the cylinder.

Edison didn't have time to work on the kinetoscope, so he gave the job to a team of employees led by William Dickson. While Dickson and his men tinkered, Edison went to France. There he observed a scientist doing work similar to Muybridge's, except he used a roll of film to take many pictures in a short period of time. Edison decided that was the key to creating a machine that would record moving pictures.

By 1891, Edison's team had developed a camera called a

The human eye and brain play an important part in creating motion pictures. The brain creates an illusion of motion when a series of still pictures is shown rapidly one after the other. As early as the 1820s, European inventors created toys that gave the illusion of something in motion. One toy featured a round piece of metal with an image on each side. By spinning it, the two images blended together to create movement. In modern films, 24 still images flash by the eye each second to give the sense of a moving scene.

kinetograph that used rolls of film. By that time, his workers had also completed a kinetoscope that could be used to view the roll of film. Image followed image so quickly that it gave the illusion of motion.

Early motion photography used a disk with multiple images to create an appearance of motion.

Edison believed that people would pay a nickel to stand in front of a kinetoscope and watch a motion picture. After all, people were already putting coins in a slot to listen to the phonograph. But Edison didn't think his motion-picture equipment was ready for the public, so he and his team kept improving it.

Finally, in May 1893, his peep show, as the kinetoscope was called, made its first public appearance. Several hundred people gathered at the Brooklyn Institute of Arts and Sciences in New York City to watch a 30-second film called *Blacksmith Scene*. It showed a blacksmith and two assistants pounding on a piece of hot metal. Between 1891 and 1918, Edison's team would create more than 100 films. Some were only a few seconds long.

Films and short movies were made in Edison's motion-picture studio. Dickson designed the building unlike anything else in the world. The outside was covered with black tar paper, and its roof jutted out at odd angles. Part of the roof opened to let in sunlight to illuminate whatever was being filmed.

The entire building rotated on a turntable to follow the sun as it

For the film in his kinetoscope, Edison turned to U.S. inventor George Eastman. In 1888, Eastman developed roll film made from strips of celluloid, a kind of plastic. The celluloid film was easier to carry and use than large glass plates, which photographers had previously used. Eastman made long strips of celluloid film for Edison's kinetoscope. A sprocket inside the kinetoscope fit into holes in the sides of the film and pulled it at a constant speed. Kodak, Eastman's company, still makes film for motion pictures.

The Black Maria, Edison's motion-picture studio

moved across the sky. Edison's staff thought it looked like a Black Maria, which was a large police wagon used to haul away criminals. So the new studio received the same name.

Inside the Black Maria, Dickson chose a variety of subjects to film. One of his first motion pictures captured an Edison employee sneezing. Other films showed dancers, acrobats, weight lifters, and firefighters racing toward hotel fires. One film featured sharpshooter Annie Oakley shooting at glass balls as they were tossed into the air.

Professional boxer "Gentleman Jim" Corbett staged a fight for Dickson's camera inside the studio. He later said, "The little moveable studio was the hottest, most cramped place I have ever known."

In 1894, the kinetograph department of the Edison Manufacturing Company became the world's first movie company. Parlors opened up in New York City where people could pay to watch a peep show. The first peep-show parlor advertised the kinetoscope as "The Wizard's Latest Invention." It was an instant hit. Huge crowds flocked to see the world's first motion pictures. At times, police had to control the people who tried to push their way inside.

Boxer James J. "Gentleman Jim" Corbett, one of Edison's first actors, filmed a boxing match in Edison's studio.

Edison began selling kinetoscopes all over the world. By 1895, his company was making an excellent profit from the new invention. Later that year, sales began to fall because other companies were making similar devices. Parlor owners wanted to show films to many people at once rather than one person at a time. Inventors were busy working on projectors that would show motion pictures on a wall or screen.

Finally, an inventor named Thomas Armat created a projector that worked well. Edison agreed to make and sell Armat's projector. Armat believed that putting Edison's name on it would bring the "largest profit in the shortest time." The machine was renamed the Edison Vitascope and quickly became a success.

Since films shown on the vitascope had no sound, Edison next tried to combine sound with motion pictures. It didn't take him long to make the

Short films were shown on Edison's kinetoscope.

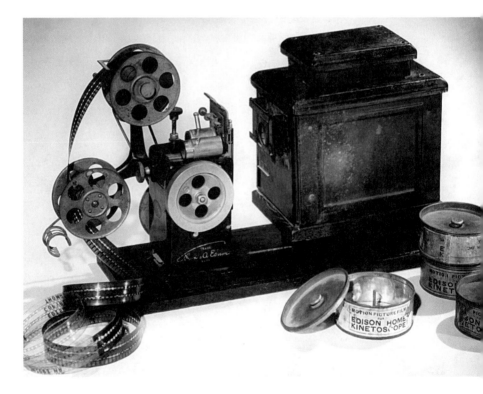

kinetophone. It allowed a person to watch a film while listening to it through earplugs that were connected to a phonograph. One of the first motion pictures with sound showed Dickson playing a violin. The technology did not work well, however, and Edison gave up on the kinetophone. More than 30 years would pass before films with sound were common.

Edison's film company became very profitable. By the late 1890s, films were telling stories rather than just capturing movement and events. In 1903, Edison's company released *The Great Train Robbery*, a 12-minute film with a plot and action that jumped from one scene to another. The story was simple, but filmgoers were astonished. The film became known as the first great masterpiece of the motion picture industry.

Over time, however, Edison lost interest in the film business. He was more interested in the mechanics of a motion picture than in its content. The public, on the other hand, was more interested in the story. Edison's film patents expired in 1915, which meant that anyone could use his ideas without paying him. His competitors had been spending more time and money making longer films with story lines, which would appeal to larger audiences. As Edison later explained, "I was an inventor—an experimenter. I wasn't a theatrical producer."

Edison was disappointed that motion pictures

became a form of entertainment. He thought the best use of them was for education. But teachers weren't using films in the classroom. "What I had in mind was a bit ahead of the time, maybe," he said. Still, as always, Edison went back to his lab, ready to find new ways to improve life. ❧

The Great Train Robbery, directed by Edwin S. Porter, was one of the first silent films.

9 CREATIVE BUSINESSMAN

❧❦❧

Since the 1870s, Edison had been interested in mining ore. For many years, he had needed large supplies of metals like iron and platinum for his inventions. On trips West, he visited mines and thought about better ways to locate ore beneath the earth.

During the late 1880s, he bought land in New Jersey and Pennsylvania and set up mining operations. Visitors to the sites commented that Edison loved to watch the steam shovels digging into the earth for iron ore. Edison told one guest that the machine reminded him of "those old-time monsters or dragons we read about in children's books." He added, "I like to sit and watch it."

To help pay for his mining business, Edison merged Edison Electric Light Company and several

Edison's workers congregated outside the mine at Ogden, New Jersey.

other companies to form Edison General Electric. Edison poured money into the ore business but struggled to make it profitable.

During the mid-1890s, he spent much of his time at his mining plant in Ogden, New Jersey. One employee wrote that Edison fixed small problems that constantly popped up, and "we worked all the way from one day to 36 hours without sleeping." Despite the problems, Edison perfected huge metal rollers to crush ore. Later, Edison would use some of the same equipment to produce cement that was used for buildings, dams, and even the construction of Yankee Stadium in New York City.

Edison's daughter Madeleine, wife Mina, and son Charles, c. 1895

Although few people knew about his mining or cement businesses, he was still remembered as an amazing inventor and hailed as the Wizard of Menlo Park. Newspapers continued to report on his activities and what his family members were doing. By 1898, Edison had six children—three from his first marriage and three from his second. He and Mina had welcomed their daughter Madeleine into the world in 1888, and in 1890,

Charles was born.

Theodore was born in 1898, when Edison was 51. The family called Theodore the little laboratory assistant because of his early interest in science and experiments. He was the only Edison child who would graduate from college. Theodore eventually did become his father's lab assistant and worked his way up to technical director of research and engineering.

Theodore Edison (1898–1992) was Edison's youngest child.

Edison's son Thomas from his first marriage got involved in several shady business deals, usually ones that promoted new inventions. Edison wasn't always happy with the way his son conducted business. Thomas' younger brother William wrote to him in 1898, "The old man says he is through with you." But eventually, Thomas and his father repaired their relationship.

As Edison got older, Mina hoped he would spend more time at home. Still, she knew Edison's work was his first passion. One magazine published an article about Mina titled, "She Married the Most Difficult Husband in America." Mina told the reporter that her husband didn't have any hobbies, and that she and her children "always put his work first." Yet Edison deeply loved his second wife, despite the many hours he spent in the lab.

At the end of the 1800s, Edison was still trying to improve old inventions such as the phonograph. But he also turned to new technologies like the X-ray. He wanted to improve X-ray equipment that had been in use since 1895. He tried unsuccessfully to take X-rays of the human skull, but he did improve the X-ray process. Edison didn't apply for patents for his work and finally stopped doing these experiments.

Since large doses of radiation from X-rays are harmful to humans, Edison developed health problems. He would later write, "Not only is my left eye badly affected ... but I am having all kinds of trouble with my stomach."

Edison didn't stop experimenting, however. Now he renewed his work with batteries, which had interested him since his boyhood days in Port Huron. For years, inventors had searched for batteries that lasted longer and were easier to use. But the development of the automobile led to Edison's quest for a better battery.

The first practical cars appeared in the 1890s. Some were powered by gasoline engines, some by steam engines, and some by batteries. In 1899, Edison began working to develop a better battery for electric cars. For two years, he experimented with metals and chemicals, trying to find a better rechargeable battery. Finally, he developed a new battery that was sometimes called an alkaline battery.

The Edison Storage Battery Company opened in 1901, but Edison took two more years to improve his battery before offering it for sale. During this time, Edison boasted to reporters that with his new battery, the price of cars would fall, and soon there would be

Edison holding the battery he invented to power his first electric car, called the Edison Baker

```
               CANADA                        N
                                          W ⊕ E
    Wash.                                     S
                                        N.H. Maine
         Montana   N. Dak.  Minn.
   Oregon                      Wis.    N.Y.  Mass.
        Idaho      South                Pa.  R.I.
            Wyoming  Dakota                  Conn.
                   Nebraska  Iowa           N.J.
   Nevada                     Ill. Ind. Oh.  Del.
  Calif.  Utah    Colorado            W.Va.  Md.
                   Kansas    Mo.       Va.
                             Kentucky
                           Okla.              N.C.
       Arizona   New       Terr. Ind. Ark. Tenn.
       Terr.    Mexico           Terr.       S.C.
 Pacific        Terr.            Miss.  Ga.  Atlantic
 Ocean                                  Ala.  Ocean
                        Texas    La.
   ▢ Coal deposits                     Florida
   ▨ Iron deposits          Gulf of Mexico
   ┼┼┼ Major railroads   0           450 miles
   ● Electrical power plant
   ● Steel plant     MEXICO  0       450 kilometers
   Map shows boundaries
      of 1900.
```

Railroads, coal and iron mines, steel plants, and electrical power stations were established during what came to be called the Industrial Era.

an automobile for every family. Edison, however, had trouble fulfilling his claims.

When placed in cars, the new battery often leaked, and after several recharges, it began to lose power. Edison and his team tried to make improvements, but Edison faced tough competition. His biggest competition was the gasoline-powered car.

In 1908, Henry Ford sold his first Model T. The car was cheap to buy and operate and easy to fix when it broke. Its gasoline engine now replaced batteries as the main power source for cars. These new cars wouldn't need Edison's battery. But Edison didn't give up on his power source. He changed his battery so it could be used to power other things like radios and lights on ships and trains.

By 1912, Edison's battery company was making a good profit. That year, Edison turned 65. His health was not always the best, but the inventor was not ready to retire. In fact, he was still spending as many as 100 hours a week in his lab. He had not lost his eagerness to explore new ideas. ☙

Thomas Edison met Henry Ford in 1896 after Ford made his first gas-powered car. Ford was thrilled when the Wizard of Menlo Park admired his work. By 1912, Ford was almost as famous as Edison, thanks to the success of the Model T car. Ford once wrote about Edison, "[He] knows that as we amass knowledge we build the power to overcome the impossible."

10 AMERICAN HERO

ᕉᘛᕉ

During the 1910s, many of Edison's ideas were published in newspapers and magazines. He didn't write only about science and technology, however. He upset many people when he wrote that he believed in a supreme intelligence but not in the personal God of Christianity. Most Americans were Christians and believed in God. Some ministers spoke out against him, but Edison didn't take back his comments. He said, "I have never seen the slightest ... proof of the religious theories of heaven and hell ... or of a personal God."

Edison also wrote an article about how to prepare for war. It was 1915, and World War I was raging in Europe. In 1917, the U.S. government asked him to head a new agency that would research and develop

Henry Ford (left), founder of the Ford Motor Company, was one of Edison's longtime friends.

military equipment. Edison agreed and ended up studying and solving numerous war problems for the U.S. Navy.

Edison ran into difficulties, however. Congress refused to give him all the money he wanted. His method of tinkering and creating also was losing ground in the world of business. Research was revolving around scientists who were studying the natural world, not inventing practical items. But Edison always believed his way of doing things was right. That would lead him to make some bad business decisions.

For years, his phonograph company continued to sell music on cylinders, even after flat records sold by competitors proved more popular. Edison also insisted on choosing which musicians he would record. But his taste didn't match the taste of most Americans, and sales of music cylinders declined.

In one of his biggest blunders, Edison refused to sell radios. The first commercial radio stations went on the air in the early 1920s. Americans rushed to buy radios so they could hear music and the latest news. But Edison insisted the radio was a fad that would fade away.

Edison's refusal to change worried his son Charles, who worked for his father. Charles wrote, "I would lie awake thinking, 'How can I stop him from making these terrible mistakes?'" In 1926, 79-year-old

Edison handed over the presidency of his company to Charles, who would run it for the next 32 years.

Edison claimed to be retired, but he stayed active. In 1927, he turned his attention to rubber. At the time, all rubber came from rubber trees grown outside the United States. Edison and his friend Henry Ford both needed rubber for their products. Edison wanted to create artificial rubber. He collected 17,000 samples of plants and vines and tested them for their rubber content. When he found ones that could grow in the United States, he

One of the plants used in Edison's rubber experiments grew in Fort Myers, Florida.

produced a substance similar to rubber.

Edison might have benefited from the help of some chemists, but he had become frustrated with them. "They think they know everything," he said. "I can't tell them anything."

Exploring artificial rubber was Edison's last major project. While he worked, he was often sick. But he was convinced he could heal himself if he ate right. For several years, he only drank milk and avoided food. This diet helped reduce his stomach pains but may have created other health problems.

On October 18, 1931, Edison died at his home in West Orange, New Jersey. He was 84 years old. Americans deeply mourned his death. Newspaper reporters wrote long articles about him, and one radio network played his favorite song, "I'll Take You Home Again, Kathleen." For two days, Edison's body lay in a casket at his lab in West Orange. Thousands of people came to view his body and honor this great American inventor and hero.

President Herbert Hoover suggested that everyone in the United States turn off their lights for one minute as a tribute to Edison. Many did that, and radio stations fell silent as well. The *New York Times Magazine* wrote that Edison was the "last and greatest of a long line of experimenters who followed only the dictates [principles] of their inner selves."

The world continues to recognize the importance

of Thomas Alva Edison and his contributions to technology and communication. His long list of patents—424 for electric light and power, 199 for the phonograph, 186 for the telegraph, and miscellaneous others—is an amazing accomplishment. His inventions shaped and changed the way people live.

Edison was buried in Rosedale Cemetery in West Orange, New Jersey, in 1931.

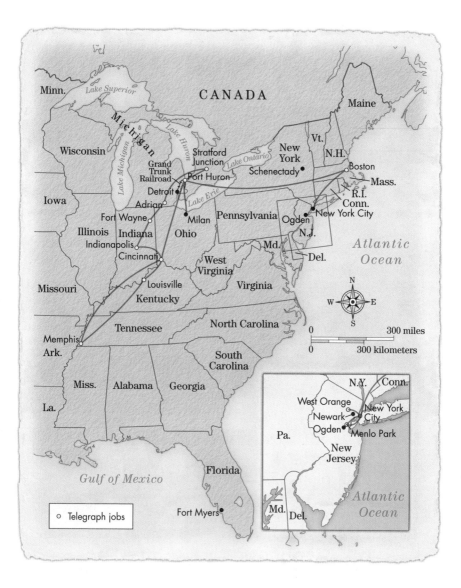

Although Edison traveled extensively as a telegraph operator, he lived most of his life in New Jersey.

His phonograph, lightbulb, electrical lighting system, motion pictures, and countless other inventions made the world a better place.

Edison also changed the world of business. By the

time he died, most new technologies came from companies that followed his example of hiring many trained scientists and engineers. Research and development became an important part of doing business.

In spite of his enormous achievements, Edison always denied that what he did was so special. He once said:

> *Genius is one percent inspiration and ninety-nine percent perspiration.*

Edison believed in himself, his ideas, and his employees. He wanted to make life easier for people everywhere, and he spent his life doing just that. The world will always be grateful for this great American inventor and businessman. ℘

In 1963, the bodies of Edison and his second wife Mina were moved from Rosedale Cemetery in West Orange, New Jersey, and reburied on the grounds of Glenmont, their last home in West Orange. Edison's first wife Mary is buried along with the couple's two oldest children, Marion and Thomas Alva Jr., in Fairmont Cemetery in Newark, New Jersey.

EDISON'S LIFE

1859

Works as a newsboy on the Grand Trunk Railway

1847

Born in Milan, Ohio, February 11

1868

Applies for his first patent for an electric vote recorder

1865

1848

The Communist Manifesto by German writer Karl Marx is widely distributed

1859

A Tale Of Two Cities by Charles Dickens is published

1869

The periodic table of elements is invented by Dimitri Mendeleyev

WORLD EVENTS

1871

Marries
Mary Stilwell

1876

Opens his
laboratory in
Menlo Park,
New Jersey

1877

Creates an
improved
transmitter for
the telephone
and invents the
phonograph

1875

1873

Ivy League
schools
draw up
the first
rules for
American
football

1876

Alexander
Graham Bell
makes the
first success-
ful telephone
transmission

1877

German inventor
Nikolaus A. Otto
works on what
will become the
internal combus-
tion engine for
automobiles

EDISON'S LIFE

1879

Develops a
successful
incandescent
lightbulb

1882

Develops the
first electric
power station

1884

Wife Mary dies

1880

1881

Booker T.
Washington
founds Tuskegee
Institute

1884

The first practical
fountain pen is
invented by
American Lewis
Edson Waterman

WORLD EVENTS

1886

Marries Mina Miller; moves to West Orange, New Jersey, and builds a larger laboratory

1889

Creates Edison General Electric by merging several companies

1893

Displays the kinetoscope, which plays motion pictures

1890

1886

Grover Cleveland dedicates the Statue of Liberty in New York, a gift from the people of France

1890

The Sherman Anti-Trust Act becomes U.S. law

1893

Women gain voting privileges in New Zealand, the first country to take such a step

EDISON'S LIFE

1895

Experiments with X-rays

1901

Establishes the Edison Storage Battery Company and continues to perfect the alkaline battery

1910

Merges most of his companies into Thomas Alva Edison, Incorporated

1900

1896

The first modern Olympic Games are held

1901

Britain's Queen Victoria dies

1909

The National Association for the Advancement of Colored People (NAACP) is founded

WORLD EVENTS

1927
Experiments with artificial rubber

1931
Dies in West Orange, New Jersey, October 18

1911
Incorporates Thomas A. Edison, Inc.

1925

1916
German-born physicist Albert Einstein publishes his general theory of relativity

1926
Impressionist painters Claude Monet and Mary Cassat die

1929
The U.S. stock market crashes, and severe world-wide economic depression sets in

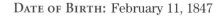
DATE OF BIRTH: February 11, 1847

BIRTHPLACE: Milan, Ohio

FATHER: Samuel Ogden Edison (1804–1896)

MOTHER: Nancy Mathews Elliot Edison (1810–1871)

SIBLINGS: Marion, William, Harriet, Carlile, Samuel, Eliza

FIRST SPOUSE: Mary Stilwell Edison (1855–1884)

DATE OF MARRIAGE: December 25, 1871

CHILDREN: Marion Estelle Edison Oeser (1873–1965) Thomas Alva Edison Jr. (1876–1935) William Leslie Edison (1878–1937)

SECOND SPOUSE: Mina Miller Edison (1865–1947)

DATE OF MARRIAGE: February 24, 1886

CHILDREN: Madeleine Edison Sloane (1888–1979) Charles Edison (1890–1969) Theodore Miller Edison (1898–1992)

DATE OF DEATH: October 18, 1931

PLACE OF BURIAL: West Orange, New Jersey

FURTHER READING

Hantula, Richard. *Thomas Edison*. Milwaukee, Wis.: World Almanac Library, 2005.

Matthews, John R. *The Light Bulb*. New York: Franklin Watts, 2005.

Rossi, Ann. *Bright Ideas: The Age of Invention in America, 1870-1910*. Washington, D.C.: National Geographic, 2005.

Tagliaferro, Linda. *Thomas Edison: Inventor of the Age of Electricity*. Minneapolis: Lerner Publications, 2003.

LOOK FOR MORE SIGNATURE LIVES

BOOKS ABOUT THIS ERA:

Amelia Earhart: *Legendary Aviator*
ISBN 0-7565-1880-6

Langston Hughes: *The Voice of Harlem*
ISBN 0-7565-0993-9

Wilma Mankiller: *Chief of the Cherokee Nation*
ISBN 0-7565-160057

J. Pierpont Morgan: *Industrialist and Financier*
ISBN 0-7565-1890-3

Eleanor Roosevelt: *First Lady of the World*
ISBN 0-7565-0992-0

Franklin Delano Roosevelt: *The New Deal President*
ISBN 0-7565-1586-6

Elizabeth Cady Stanton: *Social Reformer*
ISBN 0-7565-0990-4

Gloria Steinem: *Champion of Women's Rights*
ISBN 0-7565-1587-4

Amy Tan: *Writer and Storyteller*
ISBN 0-7565-1876-8

Booker T. Washington: *Innovative Educator*
ISBN 0-7565-1881-4

ON THE WEB

For more information on *Thomas Alva Edison*, use FactHound.

1. Go to *www.facthound.com*
2. Type in this book ID: 0756518849
3. Click on the *Fetch It* button.

FactHound will find the best Web sites for you.

HISTORIC SITES

Edison National Historic Site
Main Street and Lakeside Avenue
West Orange, NJ 07052
973/736-0551
The site of Edison's home and laboratory

The Henry Ford Museum–Menlo Park Laboratory
20900 Oakwood Blvd.
Dearborn, MI 48124-4088
313/982-6001
A reconstruction of Edison's original "invention factory"

diaphragm
a thin piece of material that vibrates when struck

electromagnet
a magnet that is temporarily magnetized by an electric current

incandescent
producing light as a consequence of being heated to a high temperature

investors
people who put money into a company so they can make more money in the future

patent
an exclusive right granted by a government to an inventor to make or sell an invention

phonograph
also called a record player; a device that plays sounds recorded on a cylinder (originally) or a record

stencil
a material that is cut into and used for printing many copies of the original

strike
a work stoppage by employees as a protest against an employer

transmitter
a device that converts sound waves to electrical impulses

union
an organization of workers set up to improve working conditions and wages

Chapter 1

Page 9, line 12: "The History of the Edison Cylinder Phonograph." 12 Jan. 2006. http://inventors.about.com/library/inventors/bledisondiscphpgraph.htm

Page 10, line 9: James Baird McClure, ed. *Edison and His Inventions*. Chicago: Rhodes & McClure, 1879, p. 77.

Page 11, line 11: Ibid., p. 81.

Chapter 2

Page 17, line 6: Paul B. Israel. *Edison: A Life of Invention*. New York: John Wiley, 1998, p. 7.

Page 20, line 15: Dagobert D. Runes, ed. *The Diary and Sundry Observations of Thomas Alva Edison*. New York: Philosophical Library, 1948, pp. 44, 48.

Page 23, line 10: Ibid., p. 19.

Chapter 3

Page 30, line 17: Reese Jenkins, et al., eds. *The Papers of Thomas A. Edison*. Volume 1. Baltimore: Johns Hopkins University Press, 1989, p. 58.

Page 30, line 22: Matthew Josephson. *Edison: A Biography*. New York: John Wiley, 1992, p. 59.

Page 33, line 24: *The Papers of Thomas A. Edison*. Volume 1, p. 111.

Chapter 4

Page 37, line 6: *Edison: A Biography*, p. 81.

Page 37, line 13: *The Papers of Thomas A. Edison*. Volume 1, p. 212.

Page 38, line 5: *Edison: A Biography*, p. 101.

Page 38, line 11: Ibid.

Chapter 5

Page 44, line 14: Ibid., pp. 133–134.

Page 45, line 4: "The Film and More." 24 April 2006. www.pbs.org/wgbh/amex/edison/filmmore/transcript

Page 45, line 23: Francis Jehl. *Menlo Park Reminiscences*. Volume 1. Dearborn, Mich.: Edison Institute, 1936, p. 10.

Page 47, sidebar: "Mr. Watson—come here!" 24 April 2006. www.loc.gov/exhibits/treasures/trr002.html

Page 48, line 3: *Edison: A Biography*, p. 143.

Page 49, line 3: *The Papers of Thomas A. Edison*. Volume 3, p. 696.

Page 49, line 9: "Edison Recordings." 24 April 2006. www.pbs.org/wgbh/amex/edison/sfeature/songs.html

Page 51, line 14: *Edison: A Life of Invention*, p. 147.

Page 51, sidebar: "Thomas A. Edison: Unorthodox Submarine Hunter." 27 Feb. 2006. www.worldwar1.com/sfedsub.htm

Chapter 6

Page 57, line 27: *Edison: A Biography*, p. 181.

Page 58, line 25: *Menlo Park Reminiscences*. Volume 1, p. 427.

Page 59, line 1: Ibid.

Page 60, line 16: "Edison." 24 April 2006. www.nps.gov/edis/edifun/edifun_4andup/faqs_fables.htm

Page 60, line 25: *Edison: A Biography*, p. 252.

Page 61, line 7: "Thomas A. Edison, 1884." 24 April 2006. http://edison.rutgers.edu/latimer/tae1.htm

Page 61, line 22: Vincent P. Carosso. *The Morgans: Private International Bankers 1854–1913*. Cambridge, Mass.: Harvard University Press, 1987, p. 270.

Chapter 7

Page 63, line 7: *Edison: A Life of Invention*, p. 207.

Page 64, line 18: *Edison: A Biography*, p. 290.

Page 65, line 24: Neil Baldwin. *Edison: Inventing the Century*. New York: Hyperion, 1995, p. 172.

Page 67, line 17: *Edison: A Life of Invention*, p. 260.

Page 67, line 24: Ibid., p. 261.

Chapter 8

Page 72, line 4: *The Diary and Sundry Observations of Thomas Alva Edison*, p. 64.

Page 76, line 4: *Edison: A Biography*, p. 393.

Page 77, line 7: Kenneth MacGowan. *Behind the Screen: The History and Techniques of the Motion Picture*. New York: Dell Publishing Company, 1965, p. 83.

Page 78, line 26: *The Diary and Sundry Observations of Thomas Alva Edison*, p. 64.

Page 79, line 3: Ibid., p. 65.

Chapter 9

Page 81, line 11: *Edison: A Biography*, p. 369.

Page 82, line 7: *Edison: A Life of Invention*, p. 356.

Page 83, line 21: Ibid., p. 390.

Page 84, line 2: *Edison: A Biography*, p. 419.

Page 84, line 15: "PM People: Thomas Alva Edison." 24 April 2006. www.popularmechanics.com/science/time_machine/1289096.html

Chapter 10

Page 89, line 9: *Edison: A Biography*, p. 438.

Page 90, line 26: *Edison: Inventing the Century*, p. 360.

Page 92, line 4: *Edison: A Life of Invention*, p. 460.

Page 92, line 25: Ibid., p. 463.

Page 95, line 15: "Thomas Edison." 24 April 2006. www.answers.com/topic/thomas-edison

Baldwin, Neil. *Edison: Inventing the Century*. New York: Hyperion, 1995.

Bartlett, John. *Bartlett's Familiar Quotations: A Collection of Passages, Phrases, and Proverbs Traced to Their Sources in Ancient and Modern Literature*. 16th ed. Boston: Little, Brown and Company, 1992.

Carosso, Vincent P. *The Morgans: Private International Bankers 1854–1913*. Cambridge, Mass.: Harvard University Press, 1987.

Israel, Paul B. *Edison: A Life of Invention*. New York: John Wiley, 1998.

Jehl, Francis. *Menlo Park Reminiscences*. Vol. 1. Dearborn, Mich.: Edison Institute, 1936.

Jenkins, Reese, et al., eds. *The Papers of Thomas A. Edison*. Vols. 1–5. Baltimore: Johns Hopkins University Press, 1989.

Jonnes, Jill. *Empires of Light: Edison, Tesla, Westinghouse, and the Race to Electrify the World*. New York: Random House, 2003.

Josephson, Matthew. *Edison: A Biography*. New York: John Wiley, 1992.

MacGowan, Kenneth. *Behind the Screen: The History and Techniques of the Motion Picture*. New York: Dell Publishing Company, 1965.

McClure, James Baird, ed. *Edison and His Inventions*. Chicago: Rhodes & McClure, 1879.

Montagu, Ivor Goldsmid Samuel. *Film World: A Guide to Cinema*. Baltimore: Penguin Books, 1964.

Pretzer, William S., ed. *Working at Inventing: Thomas A. Edison and the Menlo Park Experience*. Baltimore: Johns Hopkins University Press, 2002.

Runes, Dagobert D., ed. *The Diary and Sundry Observations of Thomas Alva Edison*. New York: Philosophical Library, 1948.

Science in Everyday Life in America. Vols. 2–4. Westport, Conn.: Greenwood Press, 2002.

acoustic telegraphy, 41, 46
Adams, James, 44
Adrian, Michigan, 27
alkaline batteries, 85
alternating current (AC), 64
arc lighting, 55
Armat, Thomas, 77
Associated Press, 29
Atlantic and Pacific Telegraph
    Company, 38–39
automatic telegraphy, 36–37, 39
automobiles, 84–85, 85–87

Batchelor, Charles, 44, 47, 63, 67
batteries, 84–87
Battle of Shiloh, 19
Bell, Alexander Graham, 46, 68
Black Maria studio, 74–76
Blacksmith Scene (film), 74
Boston, Massachusetts, 30–31, 65
Brooklyn Institute of Arts and Sciences, 74

carbon, 47, 58
celluloid film, 74
cement, 82
Cincinnati, Ohio, 27, 29
Civil War, 19
Corbett, "Gentleman Jim," 76

dashes, 17, 27, 33, 36–37, 44
Detroit, Michigan, 19
Dickson, William, 72, 74, 75, 78
direct current (DC), 64
dots, 17, 27, 33, 36–37, 38, 44
duplex telegraphy, 29, 30, 35–36
dynamos, 57–58, 61, 63

Eastman, George, 74
Edison, Charles (son), 83, 90–91
Edison Effect, 60
Edison Electric Light Company, 60, 63,
    81–82
Edison General Electric, 82, 91
Edison Machine Works, 67
Edison, Madeleine (daughter), 82

Edison Manufacturing Company, 76
Edison, Marion Estelle (daughter), 38,
    64, 95
Edison, Mary Stilwell (wife), 37–38,
    64, 95
Edison, Mina Miller (wife), 64–66, 82,
    83–84, 95
Edison, Nancy (mother), 15, 17
Edison Phonograph Company, 53
Edison, Samuel (father), 15, 16, 43, 48
Edison Storage Battery Company,
    85, 87
Edison, Theodore (son), 83
Edison, Thomas Alva
    acoustic telegraphy and, 41, 46
    automatic telegraphy and, 36–37, 39
    batteries and, 84–87
    birth of, 15
    Black Maria studio and, 74–75
    cement and, 82
    chemistry experiments of, 19–20
    childhood of, 17–20
    deafness of, 20, 48, 51, 68
    death of, 92
    duplex telegraphy and, 29, 30, 35–36
    dynamo and, 57–58, 61, 63
    Edison Electric Light Company and,
        60, 63, 81–82
    Edison General Electric and, 82, 91
    Edison Machine Works and, 67
    Edison Phonograph Company and, 53
    Edison Storage Battery Company
        and, 85, 87
    education of, 17, 19
    electric pen and, 45–46
    etheric force and, 41
    favorite song of, 92
    with Grand Trunk Railway, 18–19,
        25–26
    health of, 84, 92
    kinetograph and, 72–73
    kinetophone and, 77–78
    kinetoscope and, 13, 71–72, 73–74,
        76–77, 78–79, 94
    legal battles of, 11, 58

library of, 66
lightbulb and, 13, 55, 57, 58–60, 94
magazine articles about, 30, 33
magnetograph and, 35
marriages of, 37–38, 65
Menlo Park lab and, 43–44, 58–59
mischief of, 29–30, 33
Morse code printer and, 27
with Navy research agency, 89–90
Newark Telegraph Works and, 36
newspaper articles about, 92
nicknames of, 13, 15, 53
ore mining and, 81, 82
patents of, 11, 31–32, 37, 58, 78, 93–94
Paul Pry newspaper and, 20
phonograph and, 9–11, 11–12, 48–53, 67–68, 68–69, 90, 93, 94
Pope, Edison & Company and, 36
as press-wire operator, 27, 30
quadruplex telegraphy and, 38–39
radio and, 41, 60, 87, 90
rubber and, 91–92
sleep habits of, 25, 45
spirituality of, 89
stock ticker and, 13, 32–33, 35
talking toys and, 69
telegraph printer and, 37
telegraphy and, 13, 17, 20–21, 22–23, 25, 27, 28, 29, 30–31, 33, 35, 38–39, 41, 46, 93
telephone transmitter and, 46–48, 51
vegetable stands and, 19
vitascope and, 77
vote recorder and, 32
Weekly Herald newspaper and, 19, 20
West Orange lab and, 67, 92
at Western Union, 22–23, 27–28, 30
writings of, 89
X-rays and, 84
Edison, Thomas Alva, Jr. (son), 44, 83, 95
Edison Vitascope, 77
Edison, William Leslie (son), 44, 83
electric pens, 45–46

etheric force, 41

Fairmont Cemetery, 95
Ford, Henry, 86, 87, 91
Fort Myers, Florida, 64, 65
Fort Wayne, Indiana, 27

Glenmont estate, 66, 95
Gold and Stock Reporting Telegraph Company, 36
Gould, Jay, 38
Grand Trunk Railway, 18–19, 25–26
graphophone, 68
The Great Train Robbery (film), 78

Hertz, Heinrich, 41
Hoover, Herbert, 92

"I'll Take You Home Again, Kathleen" (song), 92
incandescent lightbulb, 13, 55, 56–57, 58–60, 94
Indianapolis, Indiana, 27

kinetograph, 72–73
kinetophone, 77–78
kinetoscope, 13, 71–72, 73–74, 76–77, 78–79, 94
Kodak Company, 74
Kruesi, John, 44, 49

labor unions, 67
lampblack, 47
Lefferts, Marshall, 36, 37
lightbulb, 13, 55, 57, 58–60, 94
London, England, 63
Louisville, Kentucky, 28, 29

MacKenzie, James, 21–22
magnetographs, 35
Marconi, Guglielmo, 41
Memphis, Tennessee, 28
Menlo Park, New Jersey, 13, 43–44, 58–59
Milan, Ohio, 15–16

Miller, Lewis, 65
mining, 81, 82
Model T automobile, 86–87
Morgan, J. Pierpont, 61, 63
Morse code, 17, 25, 27, 38, 41, 44, 65
motion pictures, 71–79, 94
Muybridge, Eadweard, 71

Navy, 89–90
New Orleans, Louisiana, 65
New York City, 35–36, 43, 57, 60,
    63, 67, 76
New York Herald newspaper, 61
New York Times Magazine, 92
Newark, New Jersey, 95
Newark Telegraph Works, 36

Oakley, Annie, 75–76
Ogden, New Jersey, 82
ore mining, 81, 82

Paris, France, 63
patents, 11, 31–32, 37, 58, 78, 93–94
Paul Pry newspaper, 20
"peep show." See kinetoscope.
phonograph, 9–11, 11–12, 48–53,
    67–68, 68–69, 74, 90, 93, 94
Pope, Edison & Company, 36
Pope, Franklin, 36
Port Huron, Michigan, 16, 19, 23,
    26, 30, 48, 84

quadruplex telegraphy, 38–39

radio, 41, 60, 87, 90, 92
radio waves, 41

relays, 29
repeaters, 29
Rochester, New York, 35–36
Rosedale Cemetery, 95
rubber, 91–92

Sawyer, William, 58
Schenectady, New York, 67
Scientific American magazine, 9, 51
"She Married the Most Difficult
    Husband in America" magazine
    article, 83–84
stock ticker, 13, 32–33, 35
Stratford Junction, Ontario, 25
stylus, 48, 50, 53, 68
Swan, Joseph, 58

talking toys, 69
Telegrapher magazine, 30, 33
telegraphy, 13, 17, 20–21, 22–23,
    25, 27, 28, 29, 30–31, 33,
    35, 38–39, 41, 46, 93
telephone, 46–48, 51
ticker tape, 33

Weekly Herald newspaper, 19, 20
West Orange, New Jersey, 13, 66, 67,
    71, 92, 95
Western Union, 22–23, 27–28,
    30, 33, 38, 48, 51
Westinghouse, George, 64
wireless telegraphy, 41
World War I, 89

X-ray machines, 84

Michael Burgan is a freelance writer of books for children and adults. A history graduate of the University of Connecticut, he has written more than 90 fiction and nonfiction children's books. For adult audiences, he has written news articles, essays, and plays. Michael Burgan is a recipient of an Educational Press Association of America award.

Image Credits

Library of Congress, cover (top), 4–5, 8, 70, 76, 96 (bottom, all), 97 (top right and bottom), 98 (bottom), 99 (top right and bottom), 100 (bottom right), 101 (bottom left); Stock Montage/Getty Images, cover (bottom), 2, 26, 100 (top right); Bettmann/Corbis, 10, 14, 31, 32, 52, 77, 93, 96 (top left), 101 (top right); North Wind Picture Archives, 12, 24, 28, 34, 62, 98 (top right); U.S. Department of Interior, National Park Service, Edison National Historic Site, 16 (all), 37, 38, 42, 45 (all), 65, 68, 69, 75, 80, 82, 83, 91, 97 (top left), 99 (top left), 100 (top left), 101 (top left); The Granger Collection, New York, 18, 54, 96 (top right), 98 (top left); Corbis, 20, 21, 22, 73; Courtesy of the Thomas A. Edison Papers, Rutgers University, 39; Mary Evans Picture Library, 40; Three Lions/Getty Images, 46; Rischgitz/Getty Images, 49; Hulton Archive/Getty Images, 50, 88; Minnesota Historical Society, 56; Welgos/Getty Images, 59; Museum of the City of New York/Getty Images, 61; Leonard de Selva/Corbis, 66; Picture Post/Getty Images, 79; General Photographic Agency/Getty Images, 85; Compass Point Books, 100 (bottom left); Corel, 101 (bottom right).